Acknowledgements
Translated by Jane Sutton
The publishers would like to thank Jean Imrie and Nick Tudor
for their help and advice.

A & C Black (Publishers) Limited
35 Bedford Row, London WC1R 4JH
First published 1986 Verlag Heinrich Ellermann,
München with the title 'Die Fisch-Uhr'
© 1986 Verlag Heinrich Ellermann, München

This edition © 1986 A & C Black (Publishers)
Limited

All rights reserved. No part of this publication
may be reproduced, stored in a retrieval
system or transmitted by any means, electronic,
mechanical, photocopying, recording, or
otherwise, without the prior permission of A & C
Black (Publishers) Limited.

Filmset by August Filmsetting, Haydock,
St. Helens
Printed in West Germany

> Schmitz, Siegfried
>   Fish calendar.
>   1. Fishes — Juvenile literature.
>   I. Title   II. Ritter, Jürgen   III. Die
> Fisch-Uhr *English*
> 597'.03   QL617.2
> ISBN 0-7136-2848-0

Fish Calendar

Siegfried Schmitz
Illustrated by Jürgen Ritter

A & C Black · London

What is a fish?

Have you ever looked at different kinds of fish? Perhaps your school has a pond or aquarium, or you might have seen lots of fish at a fishmonger's shop. One fish you often see in shops is the brown trout.

If you look at a trout from the side, as it is shown in the picture (1), the first thing you notice is the bright colours on its body. The trout is an agile fast-moving fish, about 25cm long. It has a stream-lined body to help it move easily through the water. This stream-lined shape is used in the design of submarines and aeroplanes.

Fish use their tail fins to push them through the water. To move forwards they wave their tails from side to side like a paddle. The side fins also help, although the fish uses them mainly as a rudder so that it doesn't lose its balance when it goes round sharp corners.

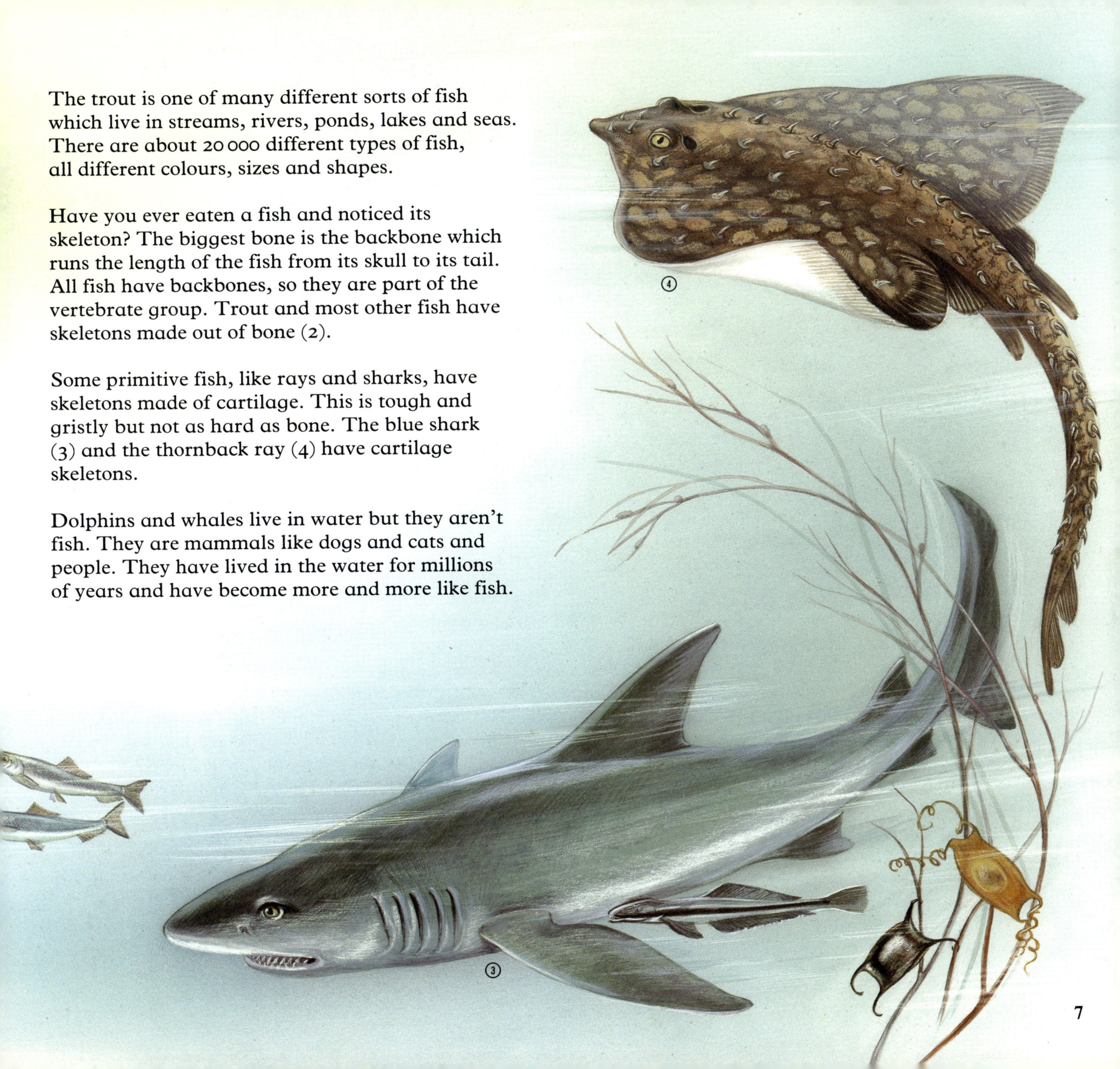

The trout is one of many different sorts of fish which live in streams, rivers, ponds, lakes and seas. There are about 20 000 different types of fish, all different colours, sizes and shapes.

Have you ever eaten a fish and noticed its skeleton? The biggest bone is the backbone which runs the length of the fish from its skull to its tail. All fish have backbones, so they are part of the vertebrate group. Trout and most other fish have skeletons made out of bone (2).

Some primitive fish, like rays and sharks, have skeletons made of cartilage. This is tough and gristly but not as hard as bone. The blue shark (3) and the thornback ray (4) have cartilage skeletons.

Dolphins and whales live in water but they aren't fish. They are mammals like dogs and cats and people. They have lived in the water for millions of years and have become more and more like fish.

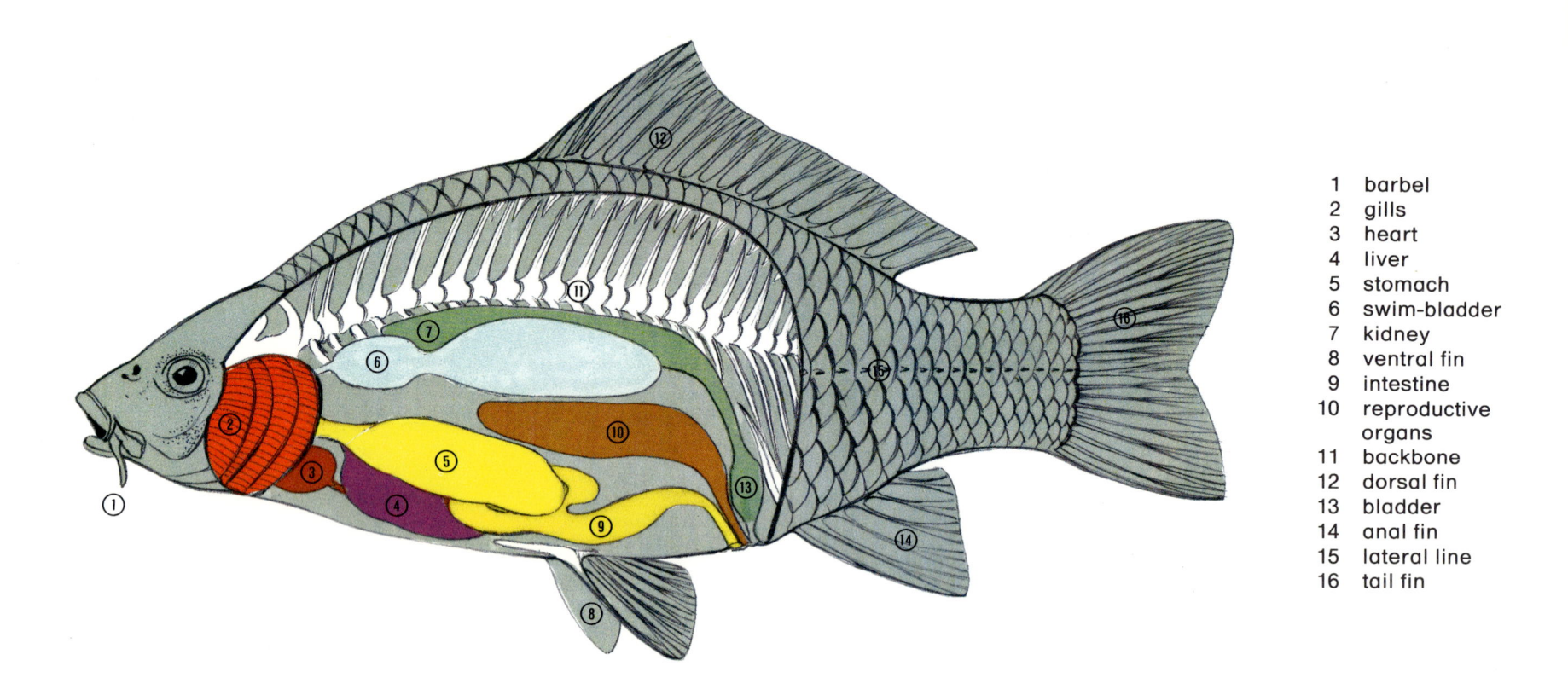

1 barbel
2 gills
3 heart
4 liver
5 stomach
6 swim-bladder
7 kidney
8 ventral fin
9 intestine
10 reproductive organs
11 backbone
12 dorsal fin
13 bladder
14 anal fin
15 lateral line
16 tail fin

Fish have adapted perfectly to life in the water. They use their fins to swim and their stream-lined bodies are totally smooth so that they can speed through the water. The skin of the fish is covered with thin overlapping scales. The skin makes slime which is a waterproof protective covering over the scales, which is why a fish feels slippery.

Fish have a special row of scales running from the head to the tail. Each of these scales has a tiny hole in it. This is called the lateral line. Water flows through the holes to the sensitive skin of the fish so that it can feel tiny changes in water pressure and wave movements. This helps it to swim the right way up and not to bump into things.

Fish can move up or down in the water in any direction they want. As the water gets deeper, the water pressure gets stronger and it could squash small fish. To stop this happening, small fish have a swim-bladder which is like a tiny balloon inside them. As the fish goes deeper, the swim-bladder fills up with gas to balance the pressure of the water. When the fish comes up again, the gas is released so that the fish doesn't burst.

Like most other animals, a fish has eyes to see, ears to hear and a nose to smell. It has a heart to pump blood round its body, kidneys to purify the blood, and a stomach and intestines to digest food.

All living creatures need oxygen. Land animals take it in from the air through their lungs. Fish take in oxygen from the water, so instead of lungs they have gills on either side of the head. They open and shut their mouths to suck in water, which goes out through their gills with the oxygen removed.

Different kinds of fish live in different levels of the water. You can tell on which level a fish lives by the shape of its mouth. Fish which live at the top of the water and find their food near the surface have mouths which point upwards (17). Fish which have mouths facing forwards usually live in the middle levels of the water (18). A fish which has a mouth that points downwards lives on the bottom (19). This sort of fish often has barbels, which are pointed bits attached to its mouth to help it find food on the water-bed.

At breeding time, most female fish lay thousands, and sometimes millions of eggs (20). The eggs and young fish have many predators, and the more eggs that are laid the more chance there is of many young fish surviving. These masses of eggs are called spawn. The male fish fertilise the eggs by covering them with sperm. Soon afterwards some of the young fish hatch out.

Most sharks and rays lay only a small number of big eggs in a hard case which is attached by threads to seaweed or rocks (21).

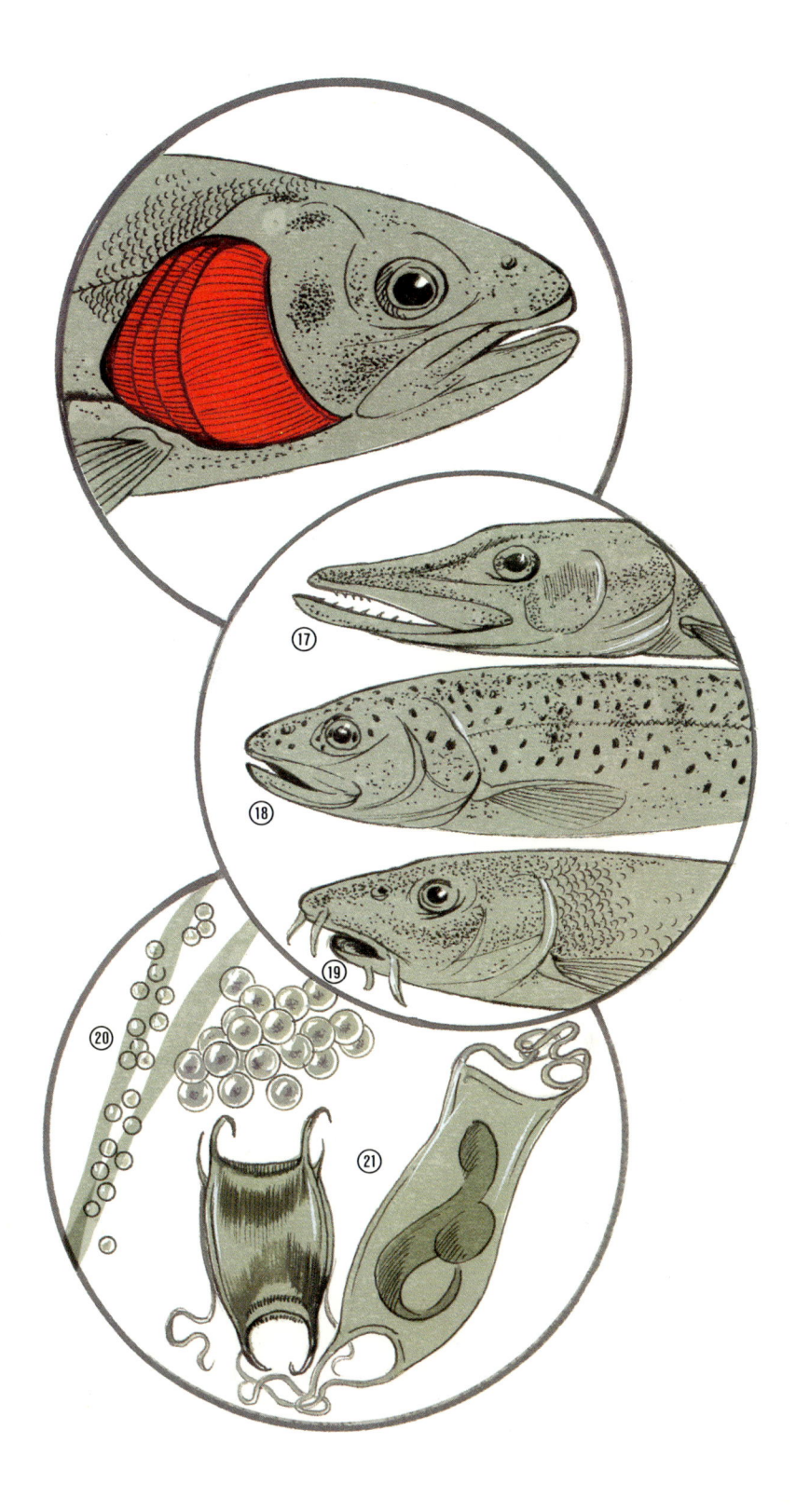

Where do fish live?

You will find fish anywhere there is enough clean water. Freshwater fish live in marshy pools, ponds and lakes, as well as streams and rivers. Marine fish live in the sea – they cannot survive in fresh water and freshwater fish are unable to live in the sea.

Freshwater fish
1. Rainbow trout
2. Grayling
3. Rudd
4. Tench
5. Catfish
6. Carp
7. Perch
8. Pope
9. Zander

In estuaries on the coast the water is a mixture of salt water from the sea and fresh water from a river. Some kinds of fish, such as mullet and seabass like to live in estuaries. Fish which migrate, like salmon and eels, can adapt to different waters and are able to swim in rivers, estuaries and the sea.

Saltwater fish
10 Plaice
11 Haddock
12 Rosefish
13 Cod
14 Herring
15 Tunny
16 Flying fish

What do fish eat?

Like land animals, all fish have to eat to live and grow. When young fish hatch out, they first eat the yolk sac of the egg. Then they have to find their own food. They look for tiny plants and animals called plankton which are floating everywhere in the water. The picture shows some of them magnified – algae, cyclops and water fleas (2).

Adult fish feed in different ways. Many continue to eat plants and plankton, or the tiny creatures which live on the bottom – snails, worms and larvae.

Fish which do not hunt for their food, like rudd (5), are called non-predators.

Other fish are keen hunters, or predators. The pike (4) stalks its prey by hiding amongst plants near the bank, then suddenly shooting out to grab the unsuspecting fish. The pike eats anything it can catch: fish, frogs (1), water birds and small mammals.

Bleak (3) and sticklebacks (6) are also predatory fish. They are all part of a food chain. The chain starts with vegetable plankton which are food for small animal plankton, which are then eaten by small fish, and so on. At the end of the chain you find predatory fish, otters (8), kingfishers (7), and people who like eating fish.

The courtship of the stickleback

The three-spined stickleback grows to 10cm long. The sharp spines on its back protect it from enemies. It is a fierce predator and eats small fish, worms and water fleas.

Most of the year, sticklebacks live together in shoals, and the males look the same as females. They are both silver-grey with darker stripes (1).

In spring, at spawning time, the male changes colour. His drab belly turns fiery red, and his sides turn blue at the bottom and greeny blue further up. These are the stickleback's mating colours (2). Now he's ready to look for a place to build a nest. When he has found the right spot, he defends it fiercely against other male sticklebacks. He uses his mouth to dig a small hollow, then he makes a loose tunnel over it with leaves and bits of plant.

When the stickleback has finished his nest, he looks for a mate. He can recognise a female that is ready to spawn because her stomach bulges with eggs (3). When she comes near, the male dances round her in zigzags and leads her to the nest. He lies on his side (4) to show her the entrance so she will swim into the tunnel. The female lies there with her head sticking out of one end and her tail out of the other (5), while the male drums on her back with his snout to make her lay the eggs. When she has laid them, the male chases her away, then he swims through the tunnel and fertilises the spawn with his sperm.

From then on the male watches the eggs and takes care of the young on his own. He stops the eggs from going rotten by fanning fresh water over them. He chases away predators and repairs the nest if necessary. After a week the young sticklebacks hatch out. The father continues to look after them (6) until they are big enough to live in a shoal (7).

Pond plants
1. White water lily
2. Yellow water lily
3. Canadian pondweed
4. Water milfoil
5. Floating bogbean
6. Horsetail

16

The bitterling lays her eggs

Bitterlings live in ponds, lakes and slow-moving streams in Europe. They like the shallow water near the bank where they can find a lot of the water plants which are their main food. Bitterlings get their name because they taste so bitter – most fishermen thrown them back. Bitterlings are small fish, growing to 9cm at most.

The bitterling's spawning time is from April to July. At this time the male becomes brilliantly coloured (7). The female changes too. A tube comes out of her body, often as long as she is (8). It is called an ovipositor and she uses it to lay her eggs. The female bitterling will only lay her eggs inside a freshwater mussel (9) so the male has to find his mate a territory with mussel in it.

Between the two shells of the mussel there is a soft body. The mussel sucks in the food and water it needs through one of its two tubular openings. The used water passes out of the other opening. As soon as the mussel opens its shell, the female bitterling quickly puts her egg tube into the mussel's breathing hole, and drops an egg into it. At the same time the male releases a cloud of sperm which the mussel sucks in with the water, so that the egg is fertilised inside the mussel. This is repeated until there are twenty or more eggs inside the mussel's gills.

The mussel is not bothered by the eggs. It carries on as normal while the young bitterlings grow inside it. The solid shell protects them from enemies, and the mussel supplies them with the oxygen they need to live. After about a month, the mussel spits the bitterlings out through the used water opening. After that they live in the water.

Fish partnerships

Predatory fish, like pike or cod (2), usually live and hunt alone, whilst non-predatory fish usually form large groups called shoals. It is safer for defenceless fish, like herrings (1) to be part of a shoal – an attacking fish often gets confused by the gleaming mass of fish bodies and doesn't know which to snap at first. Often the whole shoal can get away before the predator has found a victim.

Sometimes big predatory fish will live together happily with small non-predatory fish. The little wrasse is sometimes called the cleaner wrasse (3) because it picks tiny parasites off the body, fins and eyes of predatory fish like the grouper (4). Wrasse even swim right into the predator's mouth to pick out tiny bits of food from between its teeth. In many parts of the sea, wrasse have 'cleaning stations' where they advertise their services with dancing movements. These are so useful to big fish that sometimes there is quite a crowd of big fish, each waiting to be cleaned.

Some fish form partnerships with other animals. The clownfish (5) lives in warm seas with sea anemones (6). Sea anemones look like brightly coloured flowers but they are animals not plants. They sit on the sea bed waving long tentacles armed with poisonous stings. When a small fish comes along they stun it with their tentacles, then eat it. Clownfish, however, aren't hurt by the sea anemone's tentacles and even sleep among them, and hide in them from danger. In return for protection, the clownfish brings bits of food for the anemone.

Lakes and ponds in spring and summer

In spring and early summer, as the weather gets warmer, plants flourish on the ground and in the water. On land, fields and gardens turn green and burst into flower, and underwater there is also a lot more activity.

Fish become more lively, especially in the shallow sun-warmed areas of lakes and ponds. Other freshwater animals become more active, too. In clean water you can find all kinds of creatures. Some of them are shown in the picture.

Fish
1 Rudd
2 Mirror carp
3 Common carp
4 Crucian carp
5 Stickleback
6 Pike
7 Bitterlings
8 Weatherfish
9 Tench

Molluscs
14 Ramshorn snail
15 Pond snail
16 Freshwater mussel

Insects
17 Great water beetle
18 Great silver water beetle
19 Larva of great water beetle
20 Four spotted dragonfly
21 Dragonfly emerging from chrysalis

Amphibians
10 Smooth newt
11 Crested newt
12 Tadpole
13 Frog spawn

21

The garden pond

If you are interested in fish, you may like to keep some to look at them more closely. If you have a garden at school or at home, you might be able to find space to make a small pond.

As soon as you have put in some plants, insects and butterflies will come and explore the new habitat. The pond quickly becomes a self-contained environment.

Insects
1 Broad bodied dragonfly
2 Banded dragonfly
3 Tortoiseshell butterfly

Fish
4 Goldfish

Reptiles
5 European pond tortoise

Waterplants
6 Water crowsfoot
7 Bogbean
8 Marsh marigold
9 Pickerel weed
10 Yellow iris
11 White water lily
12 Bulrush
13 Rush
14 Arrowhead
15 Cotton grass
16 Purple loosestrife

23

How to build a garden pond

Choosing a place
If possible build your pond in a sunny spot with some trees or bushes nearby to give some shade over part of it. First mark out the site with sticks. Your pond can be round, square or any shape you like, but make sure that it is the right size for the garden – it should be at least 2–3 square metres in size.

Measuring the size
You should line your pond with a piece of plastic sheeting. To work out the length needed, measure the length of the pond and add twice the depth. To work out the width, measure the width of the pond and add twice the depth.

Making the pond
Different plants like different depths so dig your pond deeper in the middle or at the widest point, down to 80cm if possible. Leave a flat shelf about 20cm deep on one side. Smooth down the sides and bottom, take out any sharp stones and tread the earth down firmly. Put an even layer of sand 3cm thick on the bottom and tread it down.

Then spread the sheeting out so that there is the same overlap on all sides and weigh the edges down with stones. Slowly pour in the water – the weight of the water will push the sheeting down until it is pressed firmly against the bottom and sides. Cut away the rest of the sheeting, leaving an edge of 15–20cm all round. You can bury this under some earth.

Planting the pond
Now you can put in the first water plants. Buy the plants in pots and sink them onto the bottom of the pond. Put rushes, bulrushes and crowsfoot on the flat ledge with a few pond lilies in the deeper water in the middle. Then leave them to get used to their new environment.

Putting in the fish
After about two or three weeks, when the water has cleared, you can choose some fish for your pond. Goldfish are cheap and easy to look after, so are minnows and orfes. The best thing is to talk to someone at a pet shop about which fish you should have and how many. The number depends on the size of the pond so that the fish have enough air.

Looking after the pond
A pond with lots of plants and only a few fish needs very little looking after. The water level usually takes care of itself – any lost through evaporation will be replaced by the rain, although you might have to top it up if there are long dry periods in the summer. You should only feed the fish in spring after their long winter hibernation. The rest of the year they can usually find enough food in the water.

Through the winter most plants will die down until spring. If the pond is deep enough, the fish will hibernate. This is why there should be a deep area of the pond where the fish can rest protected from the cold. If a layer of ice forms across the top of the pond, you should break it in the same place every day, to stop the pond freezing completely. If the ice is more than about 5cm thick, take some water out of the pond until there is a space several centimetres high between the top of the water and the ice. Then cover the hole with a board so that it doesn't freeze again.

The migration of the salmon

Young salmon hatch in the streams in Europe. When they are a few months old, they start to swim towards the sea, heading for the Atlantic, the North Sea and the Baltic, a journey which can take up to three years. They live in the sea for a few years until they are fully grown and strong enough for the dangerous journey back. The following months are spent travelling back up rivers until the salmon reach the exact place where they hatched out of their eggs.

Eventually they arrive, completely exhausted. During the journey the salmon have changed colour from silver to purplish red and the males have developed a large hook on their lower jaws (1). With the last of their strength, the salmon spawn on the gravel of the river beds. Many then die, but some manage to get back to the sea.

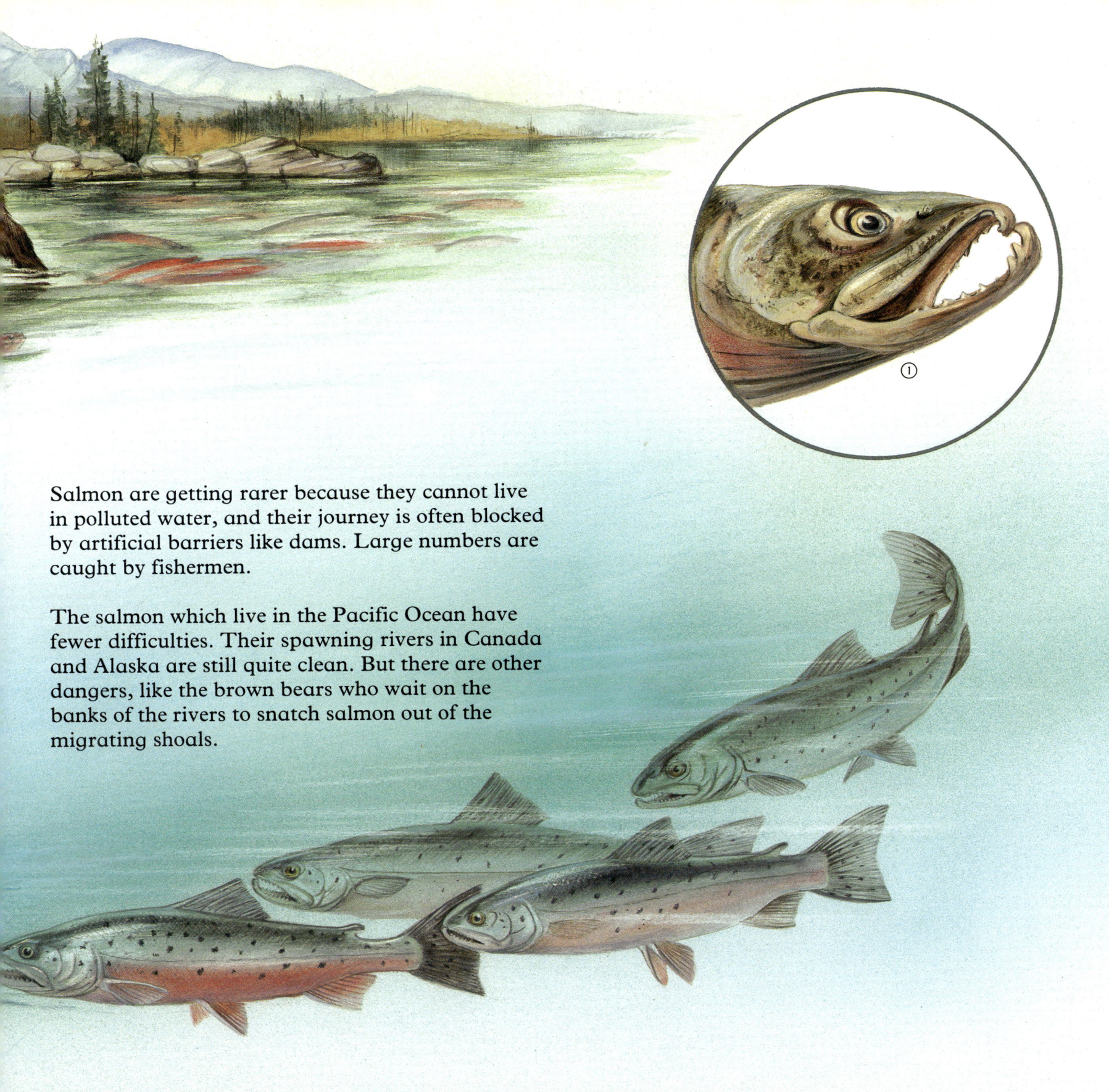

Salmon are getting rarer because they cannot live in polluted water, and their journey is often blocked by artificial barriers like dams. Large numbers are caught by fishermen.

The salmon which live in the Pacific Ocean have fewer difficulties. Their spawning rivers in Canada and Alaska are still quite clean. But there are other dangers, like the brown bears who wait on the banks of the rivers to snatch salmon out of the migrating shoals.

The migration of the eel

Common eels are long and smooth. They look rather like snakes, and live in rivers, streams and lakes. Every year in late summer and autumn, they leave the fresh water in large shoals to go on a long journey. A mysterious urge makes them swim down to the sea. Sometimes they even go across damp fields at night to shorten their journey. Their spawning ground is in the Sargasso Sea, almost 6 000 kilometres away on the other side of the Atlantic Ocean.

How eels get there is still a puzzle. When they reach the sea they disappear into the depths of the Atlantic.

It takes them one and a half years to reach their destination, and after spawning they die.

The tiny transparent eel larvae appear in the Sargasso Sea hundreds of metres below the water. They feed on plankton, growing very slowly. They drift back to Europe, carried by ocean currents. Many get eaten on the way, but millions still reach coastal waters.

The bodies of the young eels change gradually during the long journey from the Sargasso Sea to European rivers. The smallest eel larvae ever found are about as big as a letter 'i' in this book.

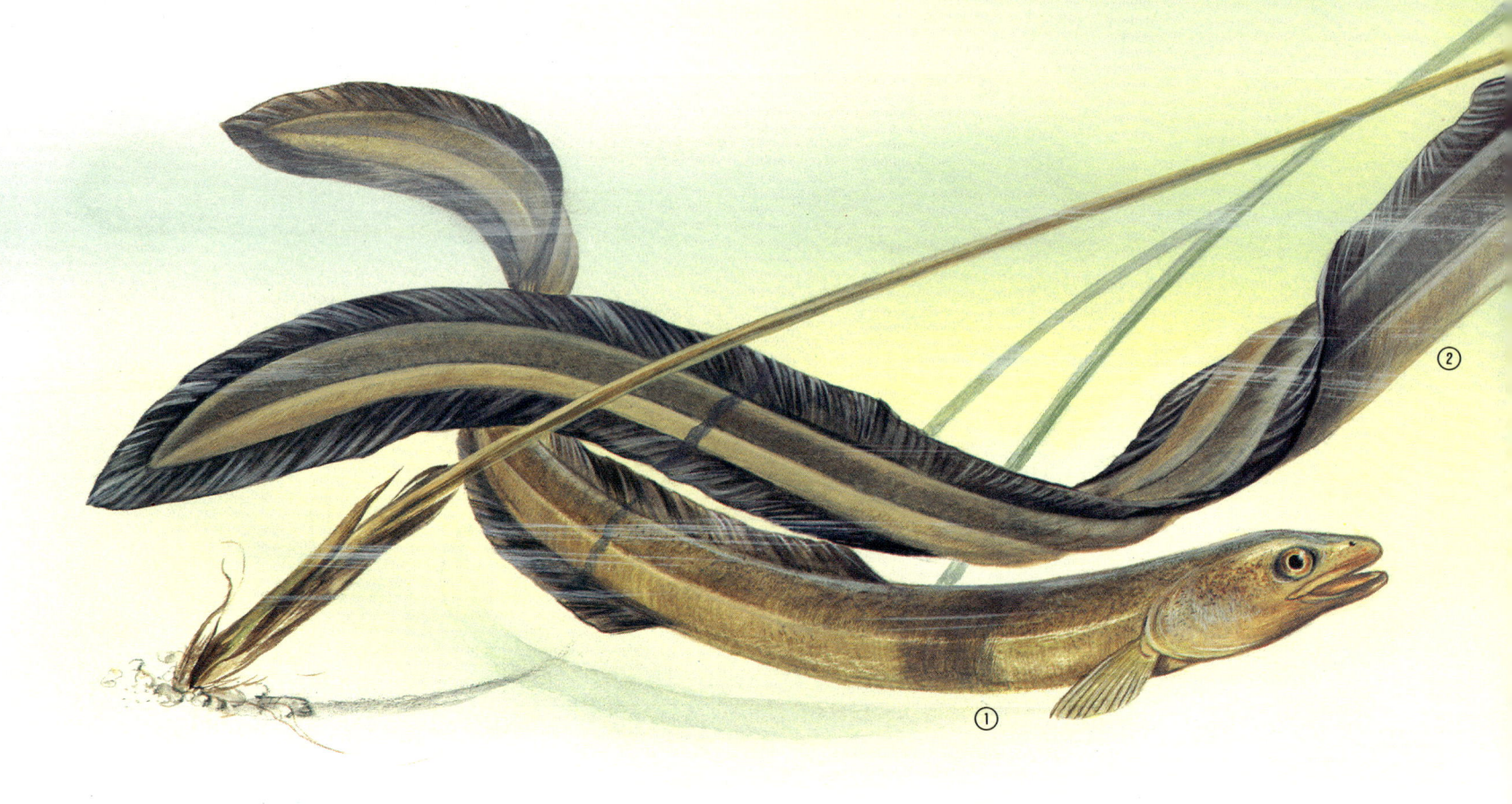

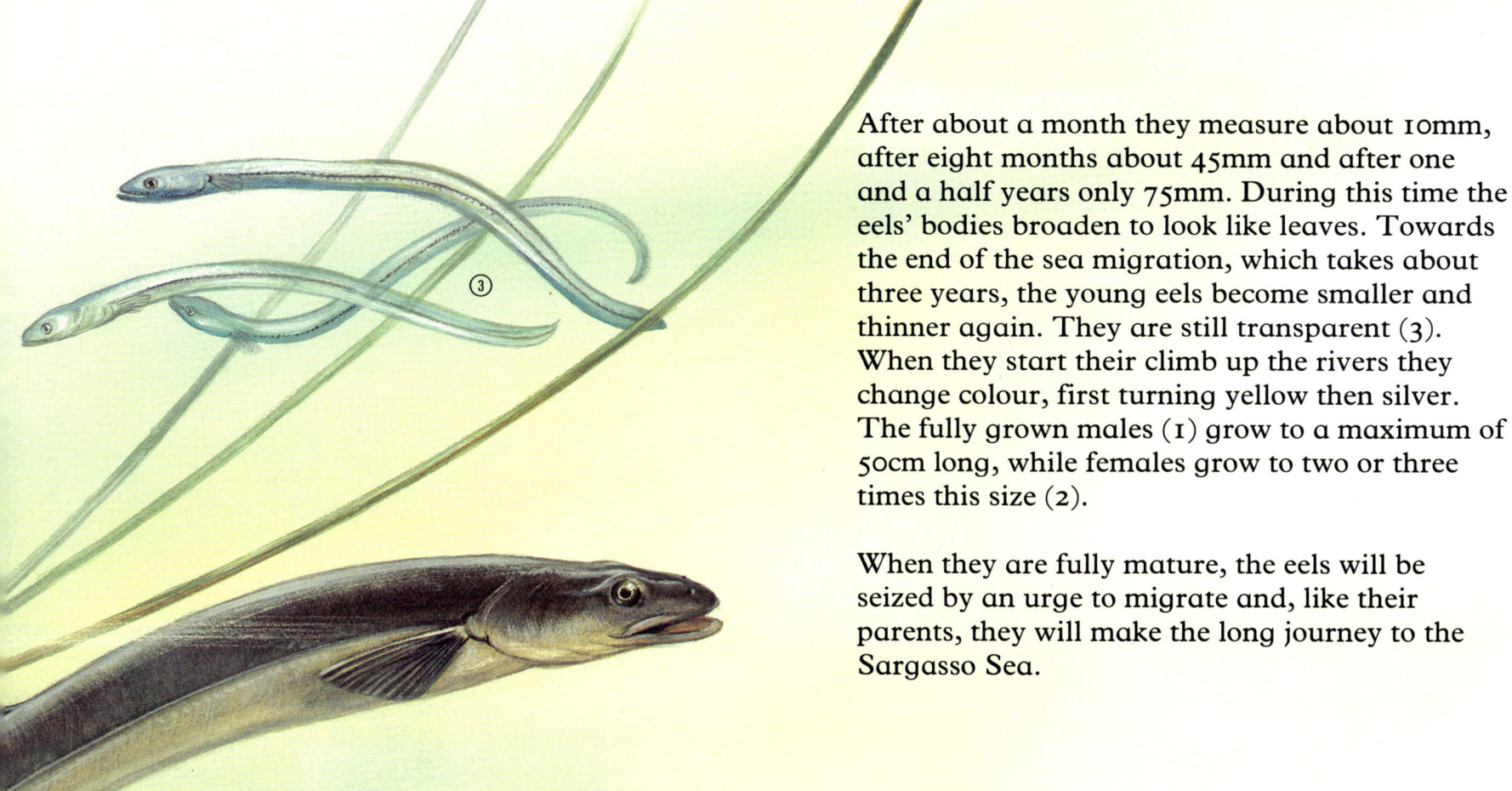

After about a month they measure about 10mm, after eight months about 45mm and after one and a half years only 75mm. During this time the eels' bodies broaden to look like leaves. Towards the end of the sea migration, which takes about three years, the young eels become smaller and thinner again. They are still transparent (3). When they start their climb up the rivers they change colour, first turning yellow then silver. The fully grown males (1) grow to a maximum of 50cm long, while females grow to two or three times this size (2).

When they are fully mature, the eels will be seized by an urge to migrate and, like their parents, they will make the long journey to the Sargasso Sea.

Changes in the young eels

Catching fish with rods and nets

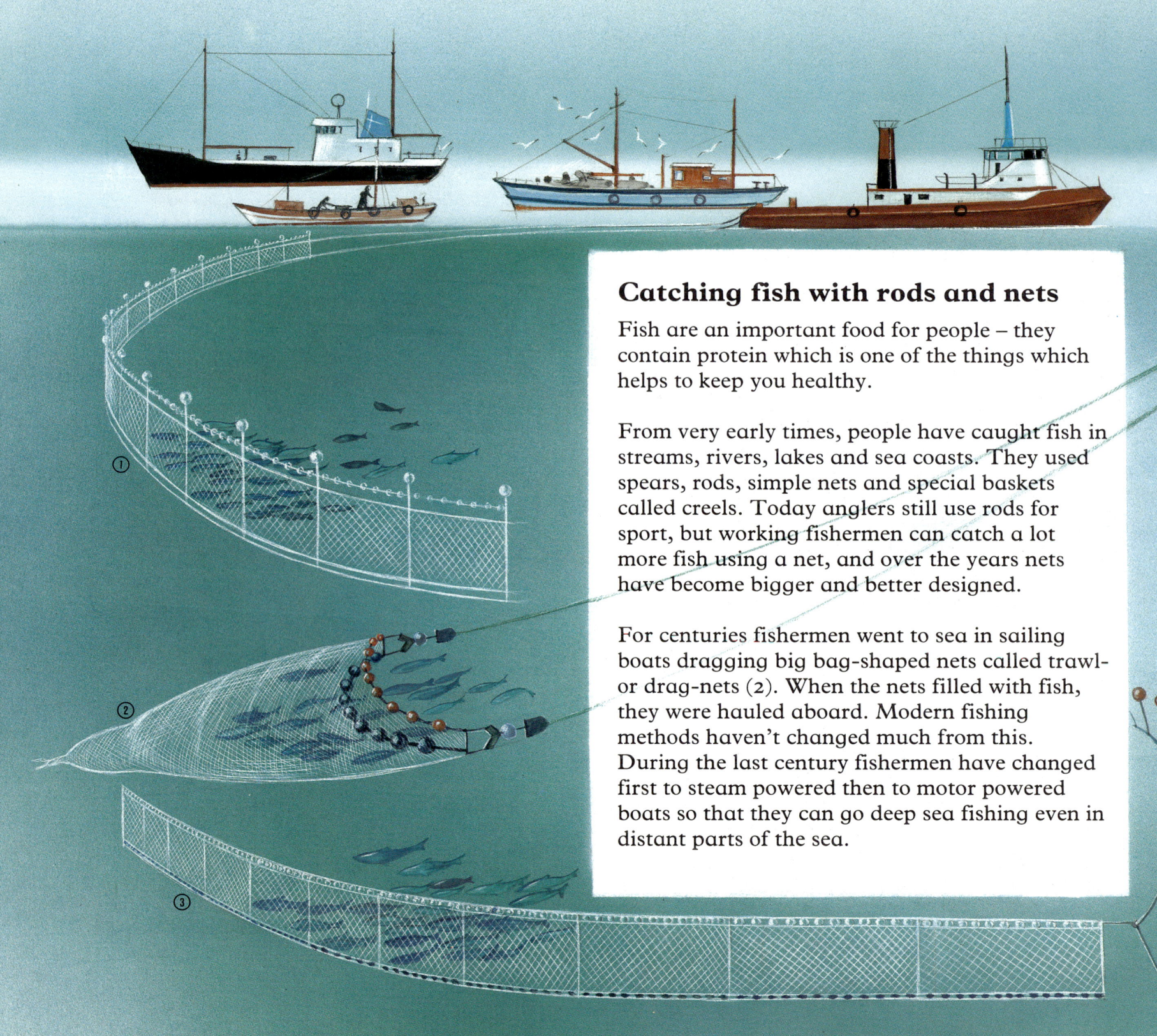

Fish are an important food for people – they contain protein which is one of the things which helps to keep you healthy.

From very early times, people have caught fish in streams, rivers, lakes and sea coasts. They used spears, rods, simple nets and special baskets called creels. Today anglers still use rods for sport, but working fishermen can catch a lot more fish using a net, and over the years nets have become bigger and better designed.

For centuries fishermen went to sea in sailing boats dragging big bag-shaped nets called trawl- or drag-nets (2). When the nets filled with fish, they were hauled aboard. Modern fishing methods haven't changed much from this. During the last century fishermen have changed first to steam powered then to motor powered boats so that they can go deep sea fishing even in distant parts of the sea.

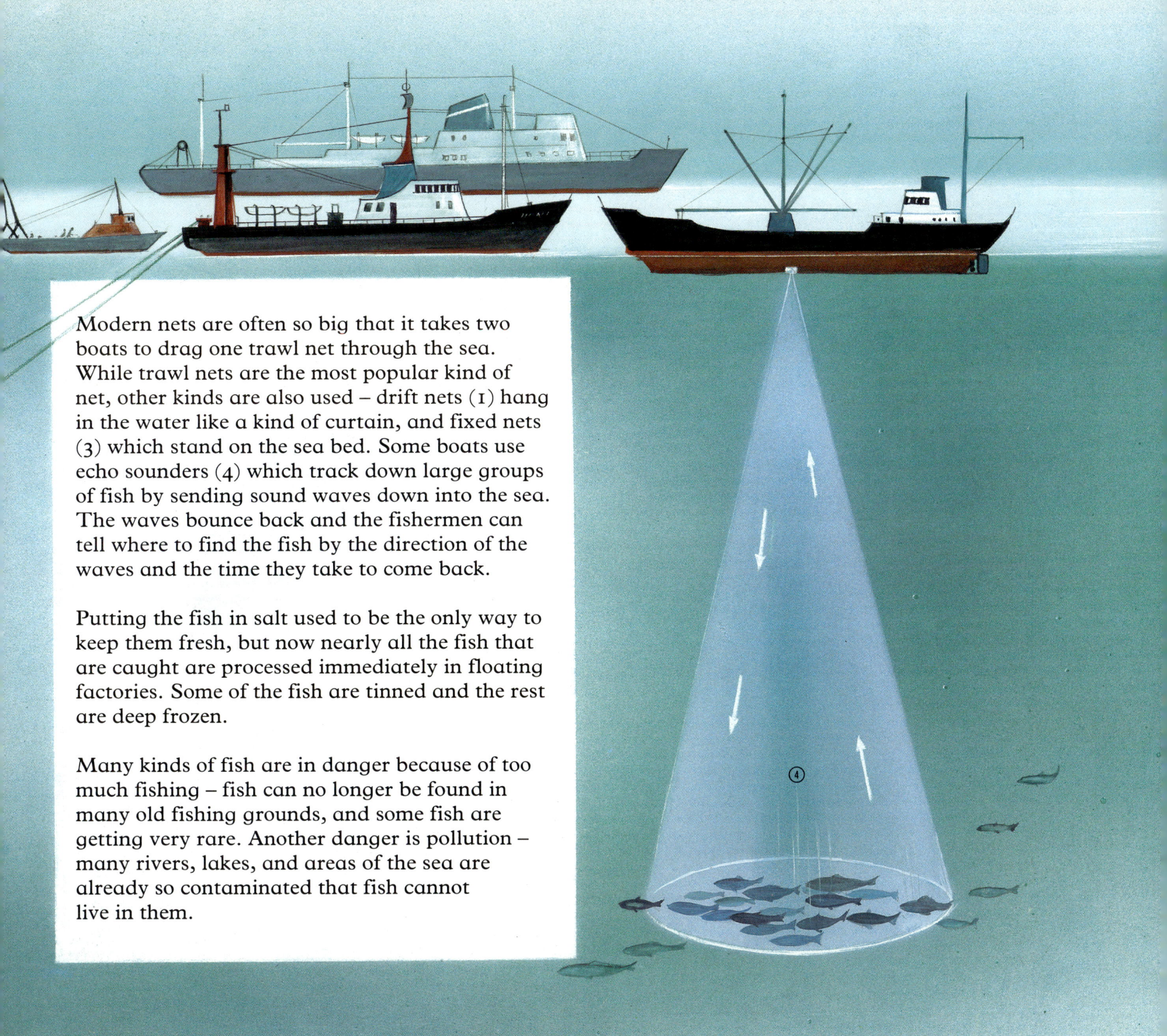

Modern nets are often so big that it takes two boats to drag one trawl net through the sea. While trawl nets are the most popular kind of net, other kinds are also used – drift nets (1) hang in the water like a kind of curtain, and fixed nets (3) which stand on the sea bed. Some boats use echo sounders (4) which track down large groups of fish by sending sound waves down into the sea. The waves bounce back and the fishermen can tell where to find the fish by the direction of the waves and the time they take to come back.

Putting the fish in salt used to be the only way to keep them fresh, but now nearly all the fish that are caught are processed immediately in floating factories. Some of the fish are tinned and the rest are deep frozen.

Many kinds of fish are in danger because of too much fishing – fish can no longer be found in many old fishing grounds, and some fish are getting very rare. Another danger is pollution – many rivers, lakes, and areas of the sea are already so contaminated that fish cannot live in them.

Fish in winter

What do freshwater fish do in winter when ponds and even lakes sometimes freeze? Most of them don't mind. Fish are cold-blooded animals so their bodies are the same temperature as the water around them. As long as the water isn't completely frozen solid, a fish cannot freeze.

Some fish suffer more from the cold than others. Carp originally came from the warm waters of Asia, and were first brought here centuries ago for people to keep in their ponds and lakes. Over the years different types have been bred – you can see some of them in the picture: common carp (1) have a full set of scales, mirror carp (2) have a few big silvery scales, and leather carp (3) have almost scaleless leathery skins.

As winter approaches and the weather gets colder, carp lose their appetites. They find a protected place at the bottom of the pond and hibernate. The carp stay together with their heads down, not moving so that they use up very little of their strength. They often don't eat anything for weeks and survive on their body fat, breathing only very gently. When spring comes, they wake up and behave as if nothing had happened.

Brown trout, unlike carp, prefer the cold. They are happiest in the ice-cold, fast-flowing water of mountain streams. Their favourite place is where the spring water comes out of the ground at a temperature of about 8°C. In summer the trout leave the streams when the water gets warm. They won't stay in streams which reach a temperature of more than 20°C. Trout territory extends downstream into the woods where thick trees keep the water cold.

Trout mate in winter. They often swim long distances upstream to find a place where they want to breed.

On the way the trout have to jump over all kinds of obstacles, just like the salmon.

When they reach their spawning place, the female trout shelter between stones while the males fight over them. In the evening they come out and use their fins to dig a small hollow in the bank. Each female then lays over a thousand eggs in the hollow, and the strongest male fertilises them immediately. The yellow pea-sized eggs stay attached to the gravel until the baby trout hatch out a few weeks later.

Starting an aquarium

It is quite easy to set up a cold water aquarium. You can get everything you need from the pet shop – a tank (the one shown has a metal frame), about 4–5 kg of coarse sand, water plants such as chickweed or Canadian pondweed, and fish.

Your tank should be at least 60cm long so that it is easy to keep clean, and standing on something stable because it will be heavy when it's full of water. Put it in a light place near a window, but not on a windowsill because the sun might make the water too hot and also the tank will get covered in algae.

Next wash the sand in a sieve under a tap until the water runs clear. When the sand is clean, put a thick layer into the tank, sloping upwards at the back.

Now fill the tank about half full of cold water. Add it very slowly and carefully so that the sand isn't stirred up. A good way is to hold the jug in one hand, and pour the water onto the other hand.

Then add the plants. Hold the roots and stem between your thumb and first finger, and press them down into the sand. Then add a few stones and fill the tank up with water, to about 5cm below the top.

Leave the tank for a couple of days so that the water clears and the plants take root properly. Then you can put in the fish. The picture shows several fish which are suitable for your aquarium. You could have some goldfish (2) or a couple of sticklebacks (5) or bitterlings (6). Perhaps you might find a mussel (4) too. Minnows or bleaks (3) would also be suitable for a cold water aquarium.

Carry your fish in a plastic bag full of water. Don't put them straight into the aquarium – hang the bag in the tank water for about half an hour so that the fish can get used to a different water temperature. Then lower the bag into the tank and let the fish swim out.

You should feed your fish once or twice a day with just a pinch of food. Never give them more than they polish off in a minute, even if they still seem hungry. Your pet shop will be able to recommend the right sort of food.

Healthy fish in a well cared for aquarium can live to be several years old. They shouldn't come to any harm if you have to go on holiday for two weeks. Of course it's safer if you can ask a friend to come in every two or three days to give them a bit of food.

A cold water aquarium doesn't need much work. A few water snails like the ramshorn snail (1) will help to keep your aquarium clean by clearing away leftover bits of food and dead plant.

You can leave the tank for years if it stays clean. It is best if every few months you take out about a third of the water and replace it with fresh water. Occasionally you will need to replace water which has evaporated.

Keeping exotic fish

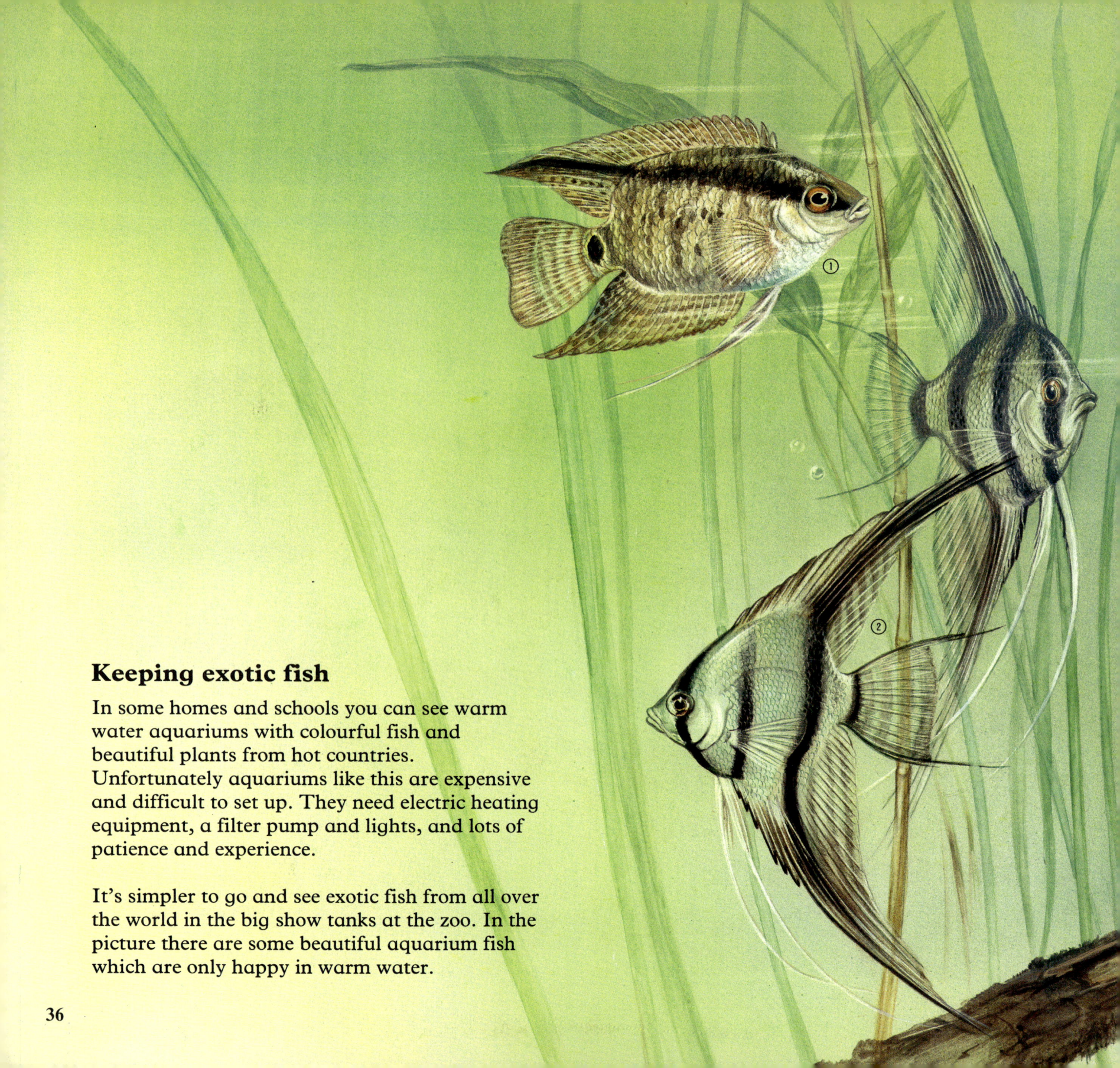

In some homes and schools you can see warm water aquariums with colourful fish and beautiful plants from hot countries. Unfortunately aquariums like this are expensive and difficult to set up. They need electric heating equipment, a filter pump and lights, and lots of patience and experience.

It's simpler to go and see exotic fish from all over the world in the big show tanks at the zoo. In the picture there are some beautiful aquarium fish which are only happy in warm water.

1 Flag cichlid
2 Angel fish
3 Nyassa cichlid
4 Daget's epiplatys
5 Black ruby
6 Discus fish
7 Tanganyika dwarf cichlid
8 African mouthbrooder
9 Nigerian mouthbrooder

Index

algae 12, 34
aquarium 34, 35, 37
autumn 28

barbel 8, 9
backbone 7, 8
bear 27
bitterling 17, 20, 34
bleak 13, 34
bony fish 7
butterfly 22

carp 10, 20, 32
cartiliginous fish 7
catfish 10
clownfish 19
cod 11, 18
cyclops 12

dolphin 7
dragonfly 21, 22

eel 11, 28, 29
egg 9, 15, 17, 26, 33
estuary 11
exotic fish 37

fertilising 9, 15, 17
fisherman 17, 27, 30, 31
flying fish 11
food chain 13
freshwater fish 10
frog 13

garden pond 22, 23, 24, 25
gills 8, 9
goldfish 22, 25, 34
grayling 10
grouper 18

herring 18
hibernation 25, 32

kingfisher 13

lake 10, 20
lateral line 8

marine fish 10, 11
migration 26, 28
minnow 25, 34
mullet 11
mussel 17, 34

net 30, 31
newt 21

orfe 25
otter 13
ovipositor 17

partnership 18, 19
perch 10
pike 12, 13, 21
plaice 11
plankton 12, 13, 28
plants 16, 22, 23, 24, 34
pollution 27, 31
pope 10

predator 13, 14, 15, 18

ray 7, 9
rosefish 11
rudd 10, 13, 21

salmon 11, 26, 27, 32
sea anemone 19
seabass 11
shark 7, 9
shoal 15, 18, 27
skeleton 7
snail 21, 35
spawn 9, 15, 28, 33
spawning 14, 17, 26, 28, 29, 33
spring 14, 20
stickleback 11, 13, 15, 21, 34
stream-lined shape 6, 8
summer 20, 28, 33
swim-bladder 8

tadpole 21
tench 10, 21
tortoise 22
trout 6, 7, 33
tunny 22

water beetle 21
water flea 12
weatherfish 21
whale 7
winter 25, 32, 33
wrasse 19

zander 11